The Dirty Little Secret About Maintaining a Consistently Clean Building

Jason Stalnecker

Copyright © 2016 Jason Stalnecker

All rights reserved.

ISBN-10: 1533001103
ISBN-13: 978-1533001108

CONTENTS

Introduction 1

Chapter 1 The Cleaning Staff 5

Chapter 2 In-House vs. Outsourcing 11

Chapter 3 Step 1 – Building A Custom Cleaning Program 19

Chapter 4 Step 2 – Training the Cleaning Staff 27

Chapter 5 Step 3 – Quality Control System 31

Chapter 6 Step 4 – Rapid Response System 35

Chapter 7 Step 5 – Adjust & Improve 39

Chapter 8 Seven Questions You Must Ask 43

Chapter 9 Conclusion 49

INTRODUCTION

My name is Jason Stalnecker, and I'm a building service contractor focused on maintaining a consistently clean building for facility managers and building owners. Ten years ago I started a small cleaning company with just three employees serving a small area in a suburb of Philadelphia, Pennsylvania. At the time, my company cleaned a school, a few churches, and three drugstores, and I focused my time on growing the company by adding more clients. I quickly came to notice that the majority of our prospective clients were saying some of the same thing when it came to the cleanliness of their buildings: "We hire a cleaning service, and they do great work for one to three months, and then everything just goes downhill from there." Most of the time, these very issues were the reason the facility managers talked with me in hopes of finding a better alternative to take care of their building. I wanted to discover a solution to this issue that so many facility managers and building owners faced, so I developed a series of systems to enable any cleaning crew to obtain consistent results each and every day they clean a building. My company now operates in four states, and we have over 60 employees.

I found that the most rewarding part of owning a cleaning service was the satisfaction of a new customer after they chose us as their new building service contractor. Their satisfaction with the end results and the processes that we utilized to obtain those results was, and still is today, the highest compliment that I can receive as a service contractor. Through my work, I help people and make their daily lives easier.

Though I have discovered a unique solution to consistent, quality cleaning results, I can't possibly personally help all facility managers and building owners maintain a consistently clean building. That's why I wrote this book to share those systems with you. Whether you have your own internal cleaning staff or outsource your cleaning, I promise that what you're going to discover in this book is going to absolutely help you get the results you desire. You can consistently maintain a cleaner building and spend no extra time doing so. Let's get started.

The Dirty Little Secret About Maintaining a Consistently Clean Building

CHAPTER 1

THE CLEANING STAFF

Cleaning is so important for any building. A consistently clean building is important to employee and visitor health and wellbeing. If employees see that you take pride in keeping the building clean, it can give them the sense that they are valued by management. Additionally, cleaning helps to maintain a professional atmosphere, which is important if you have clients that come into your offices. A clean building can improve both employee and client morale, and makes for a more pleasant working environment.

Your cleaning staff plays a vital role in maintaining your building. Cleaning staff helps building owners and facility managers clean and maintain healthy environments for the building occupants, clients, visitors, and employees. A well-managed cleaning staff will afford facility managers more time so they can focus on running their business and performing their core competencies.

You can efficiently and effectively manage your cleaning staff with a series of systems – five steps, to be specific – which work together as an effective, systematic approach to maintaining and cleaning a building. If followed, these five steps can assist any cleaning crew to consistently clean their building every day. The steps are as follows:

- **Step 1**: Develop a custom cleaning program for your specific building.
- **Step 2**: Train the staff to complete the program.
- **Step 3**: Perform quality control to ensure that the program is being completed as expected.
- **Step 4**: Use the rapid response system to take care of emergencies and other unexpected incidents.
- **Step 5**: Adjust and improve. This is where we go back

and look at and correct any issues, provide more training if necessary, and adjust the system to better ensure success.

We'll explore this five-step program in greater detail in the following chapters.

During what time of day should a building be cleaned? There are two times when the building can be cleaned - either during the day or at night. The advantages of day cleaning include potential energy savings, as well as the availability of personnel in case of an emergency clean-up. Having cleaning staff present in an office during the day sometimes gives people the perception that the building is cleaner. And with security always being a concern, having cleaning staff work during the day makes scheduling easier if you need to monitor staff in certain areas of the building, such as where confidential material is present.

Daytime cleaning is not without its disadvantages, though. Potential disadvantages include noise, interference with other staff or clients, and potentially the inhibition of the cleaning staff's productivity. When cleaning during the day, cleaning staff may have to work around offices which are in use, areas which are inaccessible, and activities (such as vacuuming) which need to be rescheduled. In short, staff may not be able to get as much done as quickly as they would if they cleaned an empty office at night.

With night cleaning, the advantages and disadvantages are reversed. Night cleaning will require that you have the lights on, which could increase the building's energy consumption. When cleaning is scheduled to take place at night, the cleaning staff will not be present in the building to meet any emergency needs that occurred during the day. This makes it important to have a rapid response system in place, which we'll talk about later in the book.

Additionally, security is always a concern when a night cleaning schedule is implemented, since you're allowing staff to go through the building without anyone else present. There are ways to implement security procedures, but it's also important to have good supervision and quality control in place. A strong manager presence can help to overcome the security concerns. Many larger buildings also have security personnel in place.

When nighttime cleaning is implemented, the presence of cleaning staff is often felt less by the daytime office staff. This can lead to a perception that the office cleaning does not take place as often, or is not as thorough as it actually is. Thankfully there are a number of ways that you can make the cleaning staff's presence. Have the cleaning staff, leave notes throughout the building, letting people know that a particular area has been disinfected. Cleaning staff can also leave other items, such as flowers or mints or candy dishes as a subtle way to let daytime staff know the area was cleaned. It's also a kind gesture to occasionally leave a thank you note to the effect of, "Thank you for letting us clean this building," accompanied by a little gift or flowers or something of that nature. These are great methods by which you can make your presence known even when you're not physically there with the rest of the staff that uses the building during the day.

One of the greatest challenges for cleaning services, whether it's an in-house service or one which is outsourced by a building service contractor, is finding the right people.

It can be difficult to find someone who is the right fit for your cleaning operation, both in terms of skill and personality. You'll also need to make sure that the person is properly trained, and when you invest time and resources into training someone, you want them to be with you long-term. We'll go over how to train a new employee later in this book.

Even when your staff is well-trained and trustworthy, they still need to be managed. Good management is key to staff productivity and to quality cleaning. Staff factors like quality control and attendance need to be actively managed. Simply making sure that staff perform and consistently show up for work is the key to ensuring that the building is clean every day.

Remember that your service's reputation rides on the work that your staff performs. If your staff is under-performing, you will be the one to receive complaints and you are at the risk of losing business. Because of this, I recommend that you test your staff before bringing them in for permanent employment. One of the advantages of being a building service contractor is that my staff perform cleaning services for multiple locations during both the day and night. This gives me the ability to test staff in different areas before I put them in a building for permanent employment. Because I've tested the staff, I know that they have the skills they need to meet my service's cleaning standards.

As we close this chapter out, I'd like to comment on one frequent complaint about cleaning companies and contractors that I hear from clients. Clients often note that when they call a cleaning service, no one answers or ever gets back to them, despite the fact that they leave a message. As a trusted partner, we need to be there, and be available, as needed. And sometimes a need arises during times when we're not scheduled to be in a building for cleaning. My clients consider my service to be very responsive, and if we're going to be a partner with our clients we believe that we need to respond quickly to them when they call. That is why you never get an answering machine when you call our company. You can get a hold of someone, and if no one's available we guarantee that we'll call back within 30 minutes, and that makes us better than all the other cleaning companies out there. It comes down to customer service, responsiveness, and reliability. And when clients realize that your service offers those qualities, they are sure to choose you over all of the other cleaning services out there.

CHAPTER 2

IN-HOUSE VS. OUTSOURCING

One of the major decisions that facility managers will face is whether to go with in-house cleaning staff versus outsourcing the office cleaning. Generally speaking, facility managers choose to clean their building using their own in-house cleaning team employed by the owner of the building or by hiring a building service contractor. In this chapter, I'm going to make the case for the latter and recommend that facility managers look to outsource rather than manage the cleaning operation themselves. I think that the benefits of outsourcing are much greater than trying to manage your own in-house staff.

What is the benefit outsourcing the cleaning? The three primary advantages to outsourcing your cleaning of your building can only be recognized if you select the right partner. In the chapters that follow, I'll provide you with a checklist to help you select that right partner.

The first advantage to outsourcing your cleaning is that you know the cleaning will be done right. Your building will be healthy, surfaces will be sanitized, and you will know that every morning when you come in, the building is going to look great.

The second advantage to outsourcing your cleaning? It saves you time. Your time is valuable, and the amount of time that is you and the rest of your company will spend in managing, overseeing, and paying cleaning staff in-house can add up quite quickly.

The third advantage involves reduced risk. Chances are, if you have your own in-house cleaning staff for your building, you are not in the business of cleaning. The best thing you can do is transfer the risk of managing and operating a cleaning staff to someone who is in the business of cleaning. For insurance purposes and for employment purposes, you are better off having someone else who is in the business of cleaning take care of your building. By outsourcing your cleaning, the cleaners that you hire are the ones that assume responsibility for keeping the office healthy and for dealing with emergencies.

Additionally, it's important to note that in many situations, the cost of outsourcing your cleaning will be less than paying in-house staff to clean. Your outsourced janitors' hourly rate will usually be less than the cost of supporting your in-house staff. In short, outsourcing your cleaning gives you more control at a lower overall cost.

One of the complaints I often hear from facility managers is that they feel that they lose control over the quality of cleaning when they outsource. This comment is generally made by managers of buildings that are looking into changing from in-house cleaning to outsourcing their cleaning. The fact of the matter is that you should have *more* control when you outsource. If you are dissatisfied with the quality of cleanliness, there are two things that you really need to look at. First, you need to identify what the real issue is. Do you have the proper cleaning program which includes cleaning frequency for your building? And are the cleaning staff performing the duties properly and with the frequency expected? Remember, you are the customer and you should be happy. If you follow the five steps that we are going to outline, you should be able to have more control over the quality of cleaning when you outsource.

Many building owners and facility managers are hesitant to outsource cleaning and state that they've always cleaned with an in-house staff which has been loyally employed for many years. This can be the most difficult aspect of considering to outsource your cleaning and change the model in which you maintain your building. This obstacle prevents many organizations from even considering outsourcing. When you hire any employee within an organization, they become a part of your team. The best advice I can give is to try and find another position within your organization for them. The second option is to offer assistance in helping your in-house cleaning staff to find other employment elsewhere. Do what you can. But the cost of an in-house model for cleaning is far greater than the hourly rate of your janitors. And recognizing the benefits of partnering with the right building service contractor can do so much more for your business.

I have one client that only hires my staff two times a year. They hire us for one week during the summer and one week during Christmas break to cover for their current in-house janitor when he takes breaks or goes on vacation. This client refuses to let this individual go because he's been a part of their team for so long, but yet they look forward to our coming in to cover for him because of the quality level of service that we provide. We clean the building far better than the janitor because we are a professional company that focuses on cleaning. There's no one at this client's facility to properly train, monitor, and ensure that the janitor does a good job.

Wouldn't it make more sense for them to allow a professional building service contractor to take care of their building properly, so that when clients come in, they're impressed by the way the building looks? Their employees will be healthier and happier knowing that the building was cleaned and sanitized properly and that all surfaces were cleaned every day. I know it can be difficult to let go of someone who has been with your company for a long time, but I think you have to look out for the long-term interest of your business.

Many building owners and facility managers think it's more costly to outsource. Usually, when I see someone do a cost comparison between the cost of a building service, hiring a building service contractor, and the cost of having their own, in-house staff, the cost of the in-house staff is solely regarded as an hourly rate. This is a mistake which overlooks the indirect costs of an employee that need to be calculated into the equation. One of these costs is the management of the employee. Management includes Human Resources, payroll, supervision, training, and more.

The second expense that is often overlooked is the cost of insuring the employee. If your business is not solely focused on cleaning or providing cleaning services, you probably have a higher insurance rate than a building service contractor would have. This has to be factored into the cost of having your own in-house staff.

You also need to consider the cost of absenteeism. What happens when your in-house staff calls out? Do you have enough people to cover for them? Or does the building just not get cleaned? Do you need to bring in outside staff to cover for them over longer periods of time, and if so, what is the cost of that?

Lastly, don't forget to consider work ticket resolution cost. When someone in your building - whether it be an employee or a client - complains about the cleanliness, the process of receiving the complaint, communicating it to your cleaning staff, and ensuring that staff have corrected the issue takes time out of both your day and your staff's day. What is the cost of resolving the work ticket that is generated by a complaint?

In the end, when you add up all those costs, does an in-house staff really cost significantly less than outsourcing? Just something to consider.

Many building owners also want to know how can they trust the staff that a building service contractor will be sending into the building. Trust can be an issue with in-house employees, just as much as it can be an issue with employees from another company. This is why it's crucial to make sure you choose the right partners when you hire a building service contractor. You need to minimize the risk of an untrustworthy staff as much as possible, and a professional building service contractor will already have measures in place to ensure that their staff is trustworthy.

When you outsource your cleaning, you will want to ensure that all cleaners will have passed thorough background checks and screenings before hire. They should also have completed rigorous company training programs. Additionally, on-site quality control and an increase in the manager's presence is crucial.

It is crucial to make sure that any building service contractor meets the right insurance requirements before they step foot into your building. Harold Soden, Sr., CIC, CRM with Oliver L.E. Soden Agency, recommends that you obtain a certificate of insurance from every prospective building service contractor. A building service contractor should have General Liability, Workers Compensation, and Auto Insurance from a reputable provider with an A.M. Best rating of A- or better. Harold also highly recommends looking for the following additional coverage from your building service contractor: Care Custody Control, a Janitorial Service Fidelity Bond/Commercial Crime Policy, and Theft Legal Liability Insurance. Care Custody Control will insure your property against any damage that may result from the service contractor's cleaning operations. A Janitorial Service Third Party Fidelity Bond (or Third Party Commercial Crime Policy) can protect your property in the unfortunate event of a theft of your property from the cleaning staff. Be aware that many bonds/policies contain a conviction clause, requiring a criminal conviction in order to pay. Theft Legal Liability, offered by some insurance providers, can afford an extra layer of protection by covering your property from negligence on the part of your contractor due to lost keys, or other liability for theft of property in their care. Coupling the bond with Theft Legal Liability provides additional peace of mind when building service employees are on your premises, particularly when you are not. Lastly, when you do in fact hire a building service contract, Harold recommends that you include a provision in your contract requiring additional insured status, and not only confirm this with the certificate of insurance, but also require a copy of their policy endorsement affording such protection. Harold Soden, Sr., CIC, CRM has 36 years experience assisting businesses in managing their risk. You can find more information on his website at www.SodenInsurance.com.

When you hire a cleaning service, communicating with the cleaning company can sometimes be a challenge. A good partner should make communication easy and should build a communication system around your needs. You are a customer, and you should be happy with the service and able to easily reach your cleaning company. With the technology that is available today, including e-mail, cell phones, and the internet, it should be easier than ever to communicate with an outside partner.

In order to best communicate with our clients, we prefer to have our clients determine their preferred method of communication, whether it be phone, e-mail, in-person, or via a log book that can be provided online or on-site. Then you can require that your building service partner or contractor is available per your preferred method. It's also important to define an acceptable and expected response time for the cleaning company. I also highly recommend that you include specific details on communication methods and expected response times in your contract with the company. They need to meet these requirements in order to get paid.

"How do I ensure the quality of service does not change after one month?" This is a common complaint that I hear time and time again when I meet with prospective clients. They say the quality of cleaning is great for one to three months, but then the cleaning quality starts to deteriorate. The key to a consistently clean building is process - having a solid process in place from start to finish and putting continuous improvement into the process. After ten years, I've developed a standard five-step process proprietary to my business and my company. You, too, can follow and implement this process, or have the knowledge to ensure that a qualified building service contractor is hired and permitted into your building. We'll look at how you can build and implement this process in the next chapter.

CHAPTER 3

STEP 1 – BUILDING A CUSTOM CLEANING PROGRAM

Building a custom cleaning program is the first step toward success for anyone who wants to clean and maintain their building on a consistent basis. Why do you need a custom program? Every building is different, from its physical makeup to its functional everyday use. The components of this first step lay the foundation for everything else I'm going to discuss in this book, and this custom program is crucial for ultimately achieving a consistently clean building.

What do you need to do to start developing the program? First, you need to fully document the physical makeup of the building. Quantify every surface and document its composition, up to and including, square footage by area. And by area you need to break down the building into each separate area that it contains. Examples of areas would be offices, restrooms, lunch rooms, conference rooms, hallways, entrances, and any other areas contained within the building. You also need to document the type of flooring in each area. Are you working with vinyl composition tile, ceramic tile wood, carpet, cement, or another flooring type? You will need to quantify the number of toilets, sinks, and showers present. You should also obtain the number of interior and exterior glass surfaces that need to be cleaned.

Additionally, you should identify all of the common contamination surfaces and areas. These are high-use surfaces which multiple people use each day. The most common surfaces with high levels of contamination include things like computer mice, keyboards, phones, desk phones, break room sink faucet handles, microwaves, refrigerator door handles, water fountain buttons, vending machine buttons, elevators, entrance doors, and so on.

These surfaces which commonly have the highest level of

contamination require cleaning every day that the building is used. The snapshot below includes an example of data necessary to capture for each area.

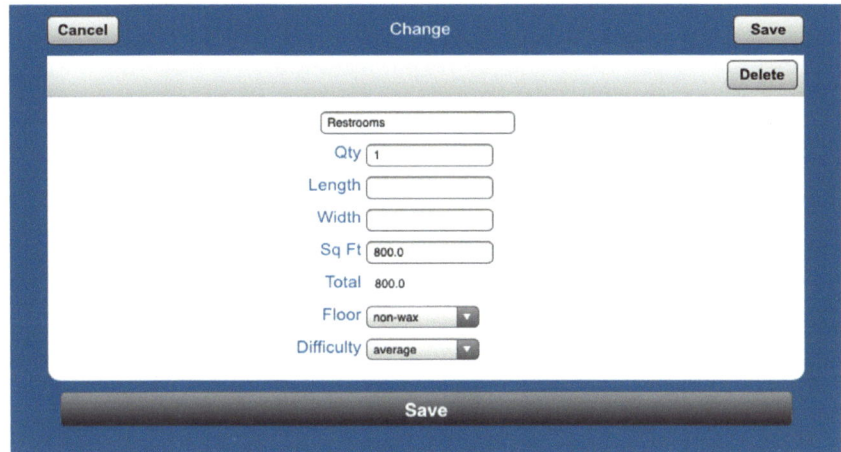

When you collect all of this information, input all the data into a spreadsheet or janitorial software program. There are multiple programs available for use that can make this much easier. A Google search will identify several available options, or you can construct your own using a spreadsheet or even a Word document. Whatever program you decide on, you're going to construct a detailed list of daily tasks and responsibilities by building area. If you have your own in-house staff, this list will serve as a daily resource for your staff, so your expectations are clearly outlined and the staff is aware of every day the work is to be performed. If you outsource to a building service contractor, then make sure this list of responsibilities is included as a requirement in your contract or agreement. Also, I recommend asking your building service contractor to detail the process they will use to ensure compliance to the daily responsibilities. You need to know that these duties are going to be performed every day. We'll talk more about how to ensure this in the quality control chapter. An example of Job Specifications can be found below.

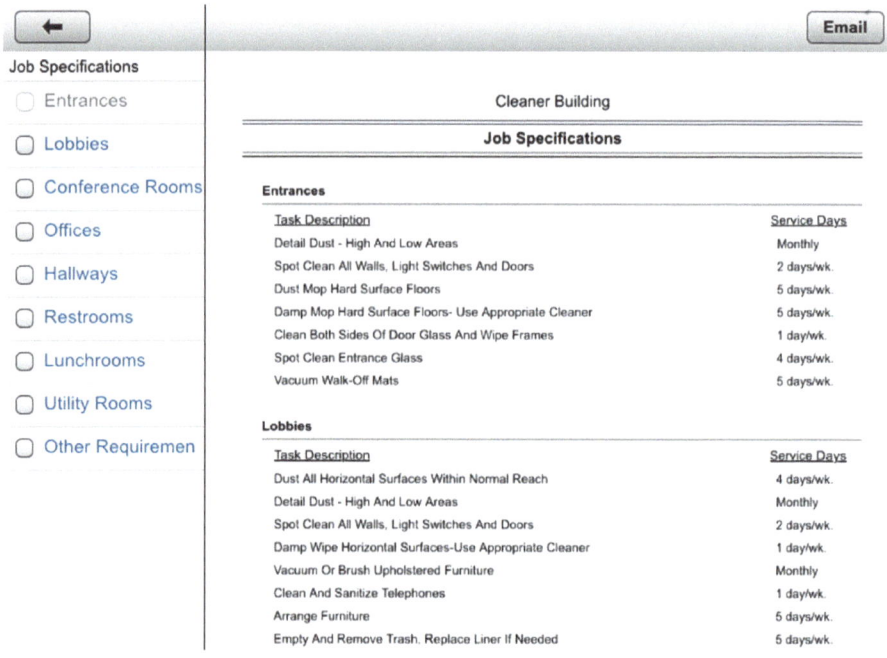

You should workload each area based on standard industry production rates. If you use a software program, information on industry production rates can be obtained at the touch of a button. Otherwise, the information can be manually obtained from one of the leading industry cleaning organizations, such as Building Service Contractors Association (BSCAI) or International Sanitary Supply Association (ISSA).

If you have some areas of the building that are used more heavily than others, it is good practice to identify these hotspot areas so you can weight them differently in your production rates when work-loading. You will need to adjust the cleaning frequency and the time permitted to clean accordingly.

The surfaces with higher levels of contamination will require special attention, increased cleaning frequency, and additional time for cleaning. Surfaces with the highest level of contamination include doors, stair railings, copy stations, elevator bathrooms, conference tables, water cooler and kitchen space, lobby reception areas, ATMs, and restrooms. According to a study by the *Kimberly-Clark Professional, Healthy Workplace Project Research Team*, these areas have scientifically proven higher levels of contamination.[1] Reduce the chance of contamination in these areas of your building by sanitizing regularly, thereby reducing employee absenteeism due to illness. As a side note, I would also recommend making sure you have hand sanitizer and sanitizer wipes available at these areas so that your own staff can be trained and made aware of the high levels of contamination in these areas.

How frequently should the building be cleaned? Any building needs to be cleaned every day it is in use, whether it is during the day or at night when the occupants have left. Many building managers say that they can't afford to have the whole building cleaned every day. My response is that you cannot afford not to have it cleaned every day. We just discussed surfaces that have high levels of contamination. Some statistics from ISSA that attest to the importance of daily cleaning: If highly contaminated surfaces are cleaned properly and regularly, the chance of catching the common cold and influenza is reduced by 80%. When commonly contaminated surfaces are cleaned regularly, surfaces contaminated with viruses are reduced by 62%, and the employee absenteeism rate is reduced by 46%.[1]

You'll also want to consider these additional statistics when considering how frequently your building should be cleaned. Organizations across the United States experience an average of 7.7 sick days per employee per year. Unplanned absences cause a 54% decrease in employee productivity and output, and result in a 39% drop in sales and/or customer service levels.[1]

If you operate a store or restaurant environment where you have customers coming into your building, a survey shows that 60% of customers said that a store's environment encouraged them to buy more.[1] This means that you can actually increase revenue by ensuring that your building is properly cleaned every day. Ninety-four percent of people said they would avoid a business if they found a dirty restroom.[1] You can't afford to have a restroom that is not up to expectations of your customers, especially in today's environment where the Internet can make something of that nature go viral on a website. For customers deciding where to shop in retail environments, cleanliness is ranked as the most important element aside from lighting, temperature, quietness in music, and special events. Clean facilities are not just an expense; they are an investment, since they can generate revenue for your business and improve your bottom line.

---

[1] *Source: "The Value of Clean White Paper." ISSA. ISSA. Web. <http://www.issa.com/value-of-clean-whitepaper>.*

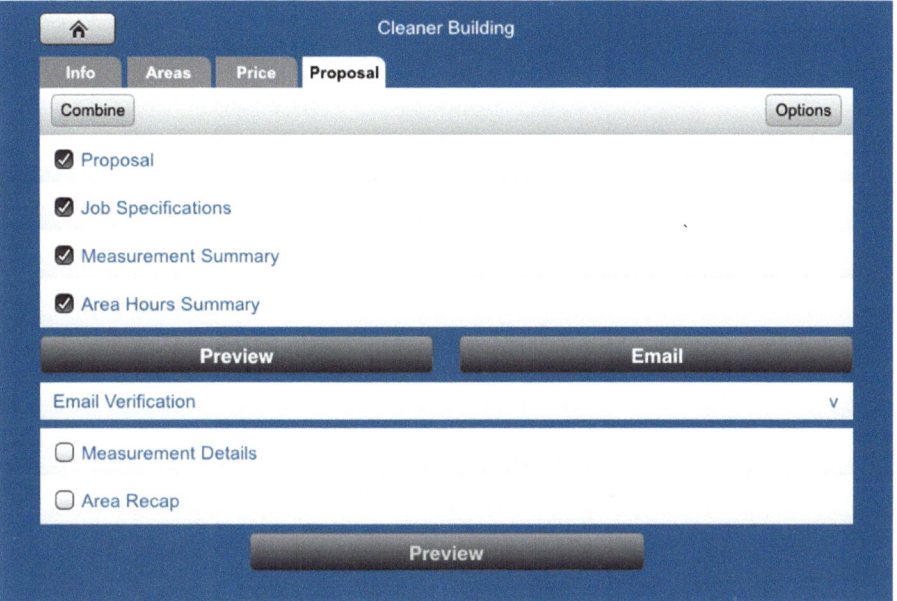

Janitorial Software can quickly provide reports based on building data.

The Dirty Little Secret About Maintaining a Consistently Clean Building

CHAPTER 4

STEP 2 – TRAINING THE CLEANING STAFF

So far you've developed a list of cleaning tasks and responsibilities. Now, each task needs to be performed as frequently as specified and in accordance with industry standards. How do you ensure this? Quality control.

By putting the staff through a specific training program, you can be sure that they have the knowledge in order to clean your building to your specifications. You will want to utilize these three top resources to put together a training program can be customized to fit your needs. The first resource is BSCAI, the second resource is ISSA, and the third resource is your cleaning chemical suppliers. The BSCAI and the ISSA are leading industry organizations that have a plethora of information from which you can get training materials from after you join. The third, suppliers, such as manufacturers of cleaning chemicals and distributors of cleaning chemicals, commonly put together training programs so that professionals who clean have tools necessary to use the products which they make. As a member of one of these leading industry organizations or customer of a supplier, you will have access to pull this training together and create your training guide or presentation for all employees to take and sign off on.

Training guides are typically broken up by area. If you have an office building composed of office space, restrooms, and a lunchroom, then you would need to match the training areas to your building. General office cleaning, floor cleaning, restroom cleaning, and lunchroom cleaning are common training guides that you can put together for your cleaning staff. If you have your own in-house cleaning staff, then you match the guides to the training areas of your building only. A building service contractor should have more general training for all areas and should reinforce the training specifically for the particular building that staff will be assigned to. This means that there should be an additional site-specific training for every building in which staff is assigned.

General training should be provided before a building service contractor sends any staff into a field. And again, site-specific training should be available for each and every client specific to the tasks and responsibilities either in the contract or expected to be performed by the in-house staff. Have the staff signoff after receiving each training. Whether you perform the cleaning in-house, or you outsource to a building service contractor, don't be afraid to ask to see proof that the training was completed by their staff.

Now that you have clearly outlined the expectations of the staff to perform each day, they need to be held accountable for actually performing the responsibilities. Regardless of whether you outsource your cleaning or not, there need to be procedures in place to track and monitor the quality of work. You can develop your own system or utilize available technology to assist in this process. Again, you can find resources for quality control technology using the industry BSCAI or ISSA websites. Many suppliers and manufacturers and distributors will also make quality control systems readily available so that you can monitor the performance of your cleaning staff or building service contractor.

How are cleaning tasks scheduled and assigned to staff? You previously created a list of tasks, responsibilities, and the frequencies in which those tasks and responsibilities should be completed. Productivity rates for each task allow us to schedule out each task with the expected time it will take to complete each area. Piece together the number of staff necessary to complete the job each day by adding up the total time expected. Scheduling the staff and assigning specific tasks to each staff member can be more of an art, but with some experience and a bit of trying and testing, it can become second nature.

Don't forget to consider the importance of safety training. If you have your own in-house staff, you, therefore, employ janitorial employees and can obtain safety training through your insurance company. They are interested in helping you be safe and avoid possible claims. Ask your insurance company to provide safety training if you do not already have a training program instituted within your organization. The training should be specific to janitorial services that will be performed by the staff that you hire. Alternatively, if you hire a building service contractor, ask them to provide their safety training manual for you to keep on record.

The last thing anyone wants is to have an incident in or around their building. Whether it's your staff, a vendor, or a building service contractor, do not let anyone begin work until you receive a certificate of insurance which includes your building company as additionally insured.

CHAPTER 5

STEP 3 – QUALITY CONTROL SYSTEM

Insuring quality professional cleaning will require tools to do the job well. Managing and monitoring consistent quality and continuous improvement into your cleaning program is crucial to the ultimate success of a consistently clean building. You've laid the foundation of work that is expected to be completed and trained the staff. Now, through quality control, you need to make sure the staff actually performs the work they were instructed and scheduled to complete.

You need to perform quality control on a regular basis. I recommend the following quality control procedure. First, rate each responsibility from step one, where you built your customized cleaning program, by an option of three choices. I find a color coded system to be easiest. Green equals good, yellow equals needs improvement, or red equals urgent attention required. Create a scoring system and acceptable scoring levels for an achievement for staff. Hold staff accountable to maintaining those levels of achievement. Rate, score, and maintain records of all the inspections. You should regularly share results with management staff to increase accountability. Then, internal training can be improved. You can create your own system for inspections or, again, utilize software that is already available. The key is to have a system that you use regularly.

My company utilizes a dynamic online program built specifically for cleaning businesses. It can also be used by other facility managers who have their own in-house staff, but the cost associated with it is more beneficial for building service contractors who service multiple buildings. The tasks and responsibilities from our step one are uploaded into the online program. We perform quality control and rate the performance of each individual task at either green, yellow, or red. Green results in no action. Yellow means some attention is required in which we give the staff one day to correct the situation. Red means that urgent attention is needed to correct a deficiency. In this case we send a special crew to immediately rectify the urgent situation that requires attention. The process of continuously monitoring the system, establishing a continuous manager presence, and checking and cycling back and retraining the staff in areas in which they are deficient creates a cycle and method of implementing continuous improvement into our cleaning process.

Our clients can actually view the results of the quality control online. They can see the progress we are making and the deficiencies that we've discovered. And when we correct those deficiencies, they are notified.

This system acts as a great communication tool recording all communication between us and our clients. This system also has a communication tool which we can use both internally and externally. Any communication that we receive from the client, whether it's by phone, e-mail, or in person, is entered into the quality control system so we have a record of everything that was discussed. When this happens, the system sends out an e-mail notification and/or text to all staff associated with maintaining the building of the client in which we are serving. This keeps everyone on the same page and provides important updates so that we may provide the best service possible.

Our quality control program generates automatic reports at the touch of a button. We can look at patterns, at individuals, and at the company as a whole. Patterns of deficiencies and patterns of areas where we do well help us to focus our efforts on training and retraining our staff as needed.

The Dirty Little Secret About Maintaining a Consistently Clean Building

Inspection Details Expand All - Collapse All   ▷ Inspection Legend
Group By: SubLocation/Section ▼   Show Tracking Item Details ☐

1st Floor - Offices, Lobby
Service Items:

100%	Empty wastepaper baskets, ashtrays, sand urns and other receptacles; damp wipe or wash liners if necessary. Haul trash to the dumpster.
100%	Spot clean door and partition glass, desks, counters and tables.
100%	Dust conference rooms, break rooms and receptionist areas. Spot dust other areas if nece
100%	Clean carpet spots smaller than one square foot.
50%	Clean drinking fountains. Remove hard water deposits on drinking fountains if necessary.
0%	Reposition all furniture correctly, turn out lights upon completion, and secure all areas as req
100%	Sweep/vacuum and spot mop stairwells.
100%	Sweep/vacuum and then damp mop hard surface floors.
100%	Vacuum all carpet in common areas and traffic ways, as recommended by the Carpet and R
100%	Vacuum under desks and tables if necessary.

1st Floor - Offices, Lobby Score:

Service Detail Score: 85% - 8.5/10

Janitorial Inspection Software scoring system for each task and responsibility of the cleaning staff simplifies the quality control process.

CHAPTER 6

STEP 4 – RAPID RESPONSE SYSTEM

Accidents happen, emergencies arise, and not all of them happen between the hours of 9:00 am and 5:00 pm. Sometimes, in the middle of the night or during the pre-dawn hours, you may need an immediate response to cleaning needs in your building. And this is where the rapid response system comes into place. During these times, you need cleaning during your cleaning staff's off-hours, whether they are your own in-house staff or a hired building service contractor.

When working with in-house staff, the only solution I have for an emergency response is to have someone on call. In this case, you're going to have to hope that they'll be reachable and available when an emergency arises.

A building service contractor should have an emergency response system in place. My company's rapid response system guarantees the following – I would suggest you use it as a guideline for any service contractor you might be considering partnering with:
- Any requests will be responded to within 30 minutes.
- All cleaning issues will be resolved within 24 hours. This would be a yellow coded issue.
- A cleaning associate will be on-site within one hour for any cleaning emergency.

Now, this is for current clients for which we clean on a regular basis. We have a 24/7 call center available at all times to notify emergency personnel, a paging system to ensure that everyone associated with the account is notified of any emergencies, and our fleet vehicles are equipped with GPS so that we can quickly find the cleaning associate who is nearest to you. No matter how you reach us, our customer support team makes sure your call is logged into our quality control system so we can follow up and ensure your request was handled appropriately, efficiently, and quickly, and that your concerns were properly addressed.

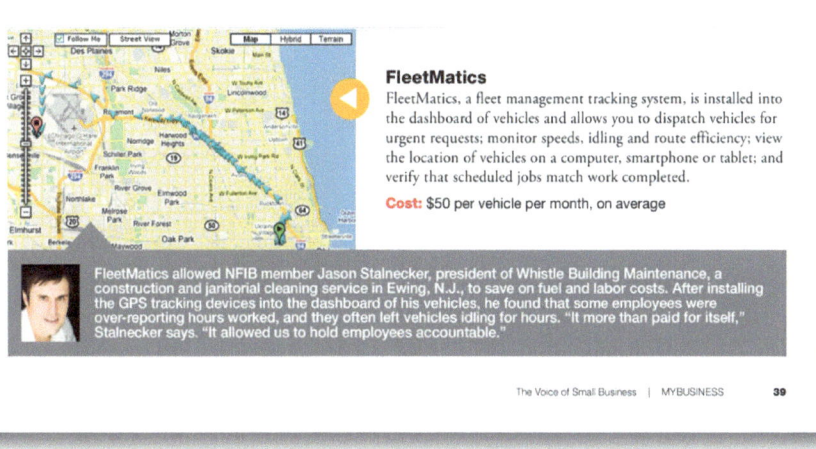

In an interview for NFIB's MyBusiness Magazine, I discuss the value that GPS fleet tracking provides to my company and customers.

The Dirty Little Secret About Maintaining a Consistently Clean Building

CHAPTER 7

STEP 5 – ADJUST & IMPROVE

You've developed your system for tracking performance and communication, and now you need to monitor results and reports so you can see where your cleaning team is excelling and where improvement may be needed. This information should be reviewed by management on a daily basis to identify the next steps in ensuring complete satisfaction. Our philosophy has always been that complete transparency in the relationship is the key to success, whether that relationship is with you and your own in-house staff, or with a building service contractor.

The five steps that I have developed are outlined in the graphic on the following page. It shows step one as the foundation of building the program. Step two is providing the training to the staff. Step three is ensuring the staff is completing the program you outlined and performing in accordance to the training provided. Step four ensures that any incidents or emergencies are covered during off-hours of the cleaning staff. Step five is to adjust and improve.

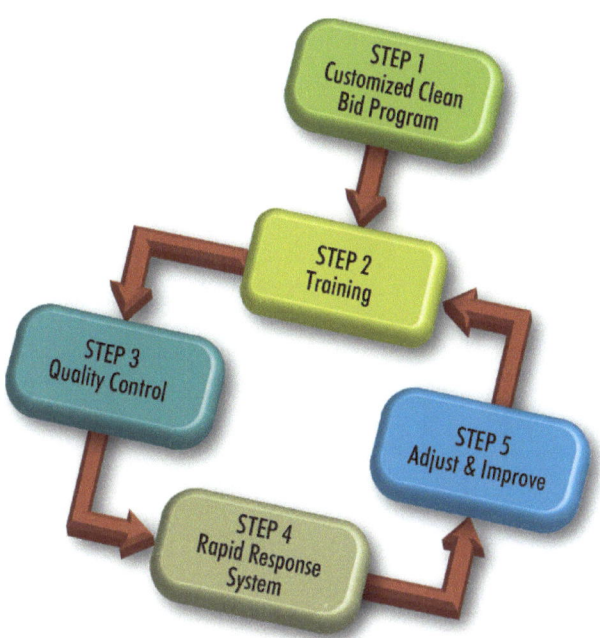

The reports and deficiencies that are recognized will help you know where to focus in with additional training. That is why step five cycles back into step two; it's a continuous improvement - a continuous cycle. A janitorial software program for quality control will allow you to zero in on specific tasks that may need improvement as well. This continuous improvement ensures top quality and great cleaning results in your building.

The Dirty Little Secret About Maintaining a Consistently Clean Building

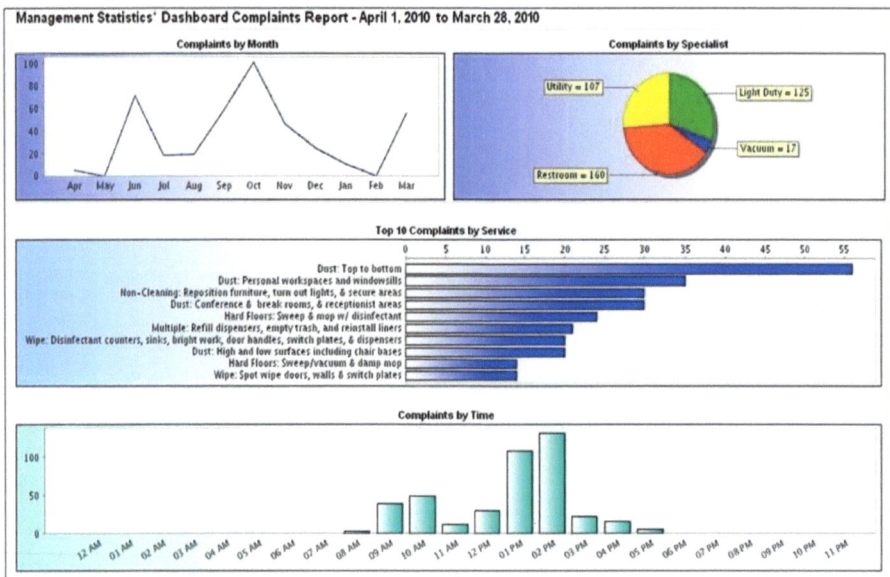

Janitorial Inspection Software can produce reports at the touch of a button to provide management with an overview of strengths and weaknesses of cleaning operations.

CHAPTER 8

SEVEN QUESTIONS YOU MUST ASK

If you are considering switching building service contractors or switching from in-house cleaning to outsourcing, then I offer the following seven questions to ask either yourself or the building service contractors you're considering hiring.

Question One: Will you develop a customized cleaning program specific to my requirements and needs in my building?

You already know how to do this for yourself. If you're looking at building service contractors to hire, any professional prospective company would want to physically see your building. If you're going through a bidding process, you should expect to take each building service contractor through your building or do it all at once as a group. Do not ask for estimates over the phone. Any building service contractor who is willing to give you an estimate over the phone based on square footage is taking a one-size-fits-all approach to estimating, and you will get in return a one-size-fits-all quality in service. A professional building service contractor will want measurements by area, as well as counts of entrances, kitchens, bathrooms, and all other highly-contaminated surfaces. They will also want a listing of floor types by area so that they can prepare a customized cleaning program specific to your building.

Question Two: Do you provide regular and site-specific training to the staff?

All staff of cleaning companies should receive a general initiation training before ever stepping foot onto a client's site. And because each building is different, they will require site-specific training for each building that they are responsible for. If you have in-house staff providing services, you will simply provide specific training to your buildings to those janitorial staff members.

Question Three: Do you utilize quality control programs to manage and monitor consistent quality?

The tasks and responsibilities you developed in the first step are available for your in-house staff to utilize, and they should be detailed and outlined in a contract with a building service contractor if you decide to outsource. How will you know if cleaning staff are performing and completing the task and the responsibilities they're expected to do? The only way is through effective quality control.

Question Four: Will you respond to any call or request within 30 minutes?

Responsiveness is one of the greatest strengths of a quality building service contractor. It needs to be important from the top down, and that is what I made important at my company. I want to be a partner of my clients, part of their team, being there when they need us. That requires having systems in place to allow us to respond right away to any requests or emergency needs they may have.

Question Five: Are you members and/or participants in leading industry organizations?

This shows the seriousness a cleaning service takes in being part of a cleaning industry community. Are you dedicated to continuously learning, improving, and training your staff in order to adhere to industry code of ethics and standards? This participation in such organizations shows the commitment of either you and your staff or the building service contractor you're considering hiring.

Question Six: Do you provide building-specific reports, including job specifications by area of facilities, and hours required by task and by area?

If a building service contractor produces these reports on the outset, this will show how much thoughtful analysis and consideration went into the cleaning program. Your ability to produce this should you provide in-house cleaning will also show the careful consideration you've given to constructing your program, detailing the number of hours on an average daily basis, and identifying the number of cleaners that are going to be required to take care of the building properly. If using a building service contractor, this should all be included in your contract so you're all on the same page regarding how long it should take, how many cleaners should be there each night, and what the performance expectations are.

Question Seven: Do you offer a money-back 100% satisfaction guarantee?

This is for solely those interested in outsourcing cleaning. If you're not satisfied with our services, and we do not take corrective action within 24 hours, we will refund your monthly fee for that month. This is our 100% satisfaction guarantee. We're not satisfied unless you're satisfied, and if we can't take action to correct your dissatisfaction, then we will gladly return your monthly fee. Cleaning services should strive for customer satisfaction, and a guarantee can indicate that a service strives to provide quality cleaning.

I have developed the preceding seven questions for any facility manager to ask themselves if they are performing in-house service, or to ask building service contractors they are considering hiring to bring into their building. If these questions cannot be answered satisfactorily, then you may not have the right partner, and you may not be ready to take care of your building and leave it consistently clean every day for your employees, building occupants, and clients that may be visiting.

The Dirty Little Secret About Maintaining a Consistently Clean Building

CHAPTER 9

CONCLUSION

The five steps I have outlined serve as the basis for maintaining a consistently clean building. My company uses this very process to service over 150 buildings in four states: New Jersey, Pennsylvania, Delaware, and New York. It may seem overwhelming, but many of you reading this may be able to take this information and run with it successfully. If you currently outsource the cleaning services of your building to a building service contractor, then use this information as a sort of checklist to guide you in selecting the right partner for cleaning your buildings. If you have your own in-house cleaning staff, then implement this system into your operation. Either way, you now have a how-to guide to help you properly and professionally maintain the cleanliness of your building.

After reading everything in this book, you may be saying, "Jason, I love what you're talking about, but how can I get this result quickly and easily?" Well, you do have some options. And imagine how you'll feel when you no longer have to deal with decreases in cleaning quality, cleaning complaints and issues, and spending a lot of your time managing cleaning staff or companies. Imagine what it would be like to put each and every one of these challenges into the past where they belong. Well, you don't have to imagine any longer. This is what I'm willing to do.

Option one is only available to businesses and organizations with buildings in New Jersey and southeast Pennsylvania that are interested in outsourcing their cleaning service operations. Call me now to schedule an appointment directly at 215-221-2870. I will personally take you through each step and will produce detailed reports, recommendations, and a plan of action for your building. This service is absolutely free, and you get to keep all of the reports and recommendations with no obligation on your part at all whatsoever.

Option number two is available to businesses and organizations that maintain their own in-house cleaning staff. I'm available on a consulting basis to get your building on the right track, but only if I feel as though it will be a good fit for us to work together. You, too can call me at 215-221-2870 so we can have a brief conversation to determine if I can be of assistance.

You can experience the incredible feeling of a consistently clean building now. Call me now at 215-221-2870. Take action on what you have discovered by reading this book. You can maintain a consistently clean building – you just need to decide to make it happen.

www.ingramcontent.com/pod-product-compliance
Lightning Source LLC
Chambersburg PA
CBHW040902180526
45159CB00001B/493